34880000823364
BOOK CHARGING CARD

974.1

Accession No. _____ Call No. FOR

Author Foran, Jill

Title Maine

Date

974.1
FOR

Foran, Jill
Maine

34880000823364

MAINE

Jill Foran

Published by Weigl Publishers Inc.
123 South Broad Street, Box 227
Mankato, MN   56002
USA
Web site: http://www.weigl.com

Library of Congress Cataloging-in-Publication Data available upon request from the publisher. Fax: (507) 388-2746 for the attention of the Publishing Records Department.

ISBN 1-930954-69-7

Printed in the United States of America
1 2 3 4 5 6 7 8 9 10   05 04 03 02 01

Editor
Jennifer Nault
Copy Editor
Kara Turner
Designer
Warren Clark
Terry Paulhus
Photo Researchers
Joe Nelson
Tina Schwartzenberger

Photograph Credits

Cover: Maine fishing village, lobster traps (Kindra Clineff), **Courtesy of the Abbe Museum:** page 23T; **Kindra Clineff Photography:** pages 4M, 4BL, 6T, 6B, 7T, 7B, 8T, 8BL, 8BR, 9B, 10T, 11B, 12B, 13T, 13BM, 13BR, 14T, 14B, 15BR, 22B, 25T, 25B, 26T, 27T; **Courtesy of the City of Augusta, Maine:** page 21T; **Kevin Fleming/CORBIS:** page 20T; **Corbis Corporation:** pages 3B, 26B, 27B; **Corel Corporation:** pages 11T, 18B, 23B, 29B; **Digital Stock Corporation:** page 9T; **Maine Historical Society:** pages 16B, 19T, 19BL, 19BR; **Courtesy of the Maine Maritime Academy, Castine, Maine:** pages 3M, 15T; **Maine Office of Tourism:** pages 3T, 10B, 22T; **Dennis Welsh/Maine Office of Tourism:** page 20B; **Maine State Museum:** page 16T; **Benjamin Magro/Courtesy of the Margaret Chase Smith Library:** page 21B; **Steve Mulligan Photography:** page 12T; **National Archives of Canada:** pages 17T (C-009000), 18T (C-13320); **Terry Paulhus:** page 28B; **PhotoDisc Corporation:** page 15BL; **Photofest:** pages 24T, 24B; **PhotoSpin Corporation:** page 28T; **Rogers Communications Inc.:** page 17B.

CONTENTS

INTRODUCTION

As the largest state in New England, Maine is something like a big fish in a little sea. The state is not only the most easterly state in New England, it is the most easterly state in the entire nation. About 500 years ago, Maine's location made it a prime fishing and trading destination for explorers. Today, fishing is still important to the area. Due to its proximity to the ocean, the state has one of the largest annual ocean catches in the nation. The fishing industry pulls in about $250 million every year.

Along with the large catches off the Atlantic coast, Maine's 3,478 miles of coastline is also known for its beauty. Its rocky shore is graced by charming lighthouses. Navigating the coast of Maine was very tricky in Maine's early days. Its many islands and rocky outcroppings made sailing the coast dangerous. There are sixty-six lighthouses along the shore.

The Marshall Point Lighthouse marks the entrance to Port Clyde, a Maine fishing and shipbuilding hub.

QUICK FACTS

Maine's state motto is *Dirigo*, which is Latin for "I Direct."

Augusta is the capital of Maine. It is the most easterly capital city in the United States.

Maine's coast has sandy beaches, tiny fishing villages, thousands of islands, and the only national park in New England—Acadia National Park.

Getting There

Maine shares more of its border with Canadian provinces than it does with other states. The province of Quebec borders Maine to the northwest, and the province of New Brunswick borders it to the northeast. Maine shares its southwest border with the state of New Hampshire, and its entire southeastern border hugs the Atlantic Ocean.

There are a number of ways to get to Maine. The state has more than 100 airports. The largest and busiest airport in Maine is Portland International Airport. For those traveling by automobile, a number of highways link the state to other parts of the country. One of the busiest highways in Maine is Interstate 95. Although passenger trains do not serve Maine, several bus lines, including Concord Trailways and Greyhound Bus Lines, bring passengers to various points in the state. Maine can also be reached by water. Ferries provide service to many of Maine's ports along the Atlantic Ocean.

QUICK FACTS

In terms of size, Maine is the thirty-ninth largest state in the country.

Portland is Maine's largest and busiest city.

Eastport is the most easterly city in the United States. People in Eastport see the morning sun before anyone else in the country.

Maine is the only state in the country that shares its border with only one other state: New Hampshire.

Maine has about 23,000 miles of roads and highways, most of which are paved.

In the United States, Maine is the only state whose name has one syllable.

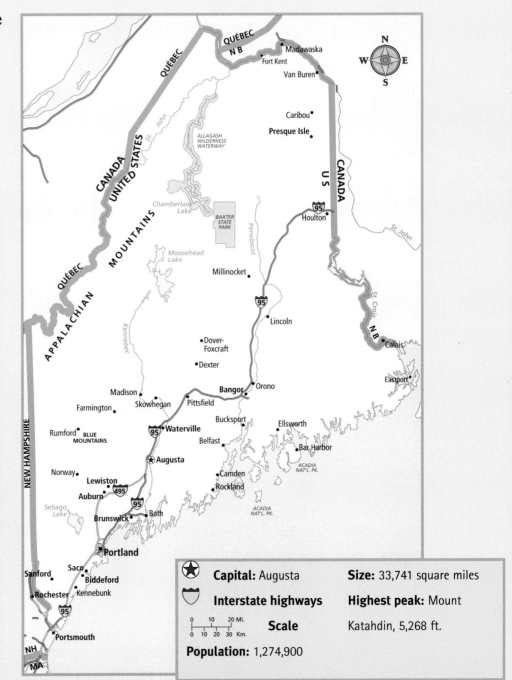

Capital: Augusta

Interstate highways

Scale

Population: 1,274,900

Size: 33,741 square miles

Highest peak: Mount Katahdin, 5,268 ft.

The Owl's head lighthouse is 30 feet tall. It stands at the entrance of Rockland Harbor.

Throughout history, Maine's thick forests and abundance of ocean life have supported the inhabitants of the area. Early Native Peoples hunted in its dense forests and fished its rivers, lakes, and coastal waters. When Europeans arrived in Maine, the region's resources helped them establish profitable trapping and fishing industries, as well as successful lumber and shipbuilding empires.

Early explorers include Italians, French, and possibly even Vikings, but it was the English who first settled the area. Several English settlements were established on the islands off Maine's coast during the 1620s. Some people believe that the name "Maine" may have been chosen to distinguish the mainland settlements from the island settlements. By the mid-nineteenth century, thousands of people from other states and immigrants from different parts of Europe had come to Maine to take advantage of its natural riches. Many came to work in mills and plants that produced goods such as paper, textiles, shoes, and food. Maine's resources were responsible for the growth of both its economy and its population.

QUICK FACTS

Maine entered the Union as the twenty-third state on March 15, 1820.

Only ten states in the country have fewer people than Maine.

Maine is home to the first chartered city in the country. York was chartered in 1641.

Maine's official state song is "The State of Maine Song."

One of the state's largest annual events is the Maine Lobster Festival. It is held in Rockwell every August.

Maine lobster is a delicacy that is available year-round.

The white pine tree, which grows in Maine, is the largest type of tree in the northeastern United States.

Maine is nicknamed the "Pine Tree State." This is because towering pine trees once dominated Maine's forests. Many pine trees were cut down in the eighteenth and nineteenth centuries for use in the lumber and shipbuilding industries. Still, Maine remains a heavily forested region. Today, 90 percent of the state is forested—more than any other state in the nation. Maine's nickname is still fitting, as there are now many second-growth pine trees in the state. Forestry continues to be an important industry, and there are many sawmills and lumber camps operating throughout the state. Maine is known for its specialty wood products, with toothpicks topping the list.

Ecotourism is another industry that is supported by Maine's natural resources. Ecotourists come to the area to enjoy the outdoors in a careful and respectful manner. Campers and hikers tread lightly on the land, making sure to pick up after themselves along the way. Residents and visitors alike work to ensure that the natural resources that have defined Maine state for centuries remain protected for centuries to come.

QUICK FACTS

Maine's state tree is the white pine. The trunk of this tree was ideal for the construction of masts during Maine's early shipbuilding days. Most of Maine's original white pines had disappeared by the nineteenth century due to the state's thriving shipbuilding industry.

Maine's state bird is the black-capped chickadee. It can be found in Maine throughout the year.

The state insect is the honeybee.

Maine's state fish is the landlocked salmon. These fish live in Maine's rivers and attract many sports fishers to the state every year. Some landlocked salmon can weigh up to 35 pounds.

Kayaking is just one of many outdoor activities enjoyed in Maine.

LAND AND CLIMATE

Maine can be divided into three natural land regions: the Coastal Lowlands, the Eastern New England Upland, and the White Mountains Region. The Coastal Lowlands is a narrow region that stretches along Maine's Atlantic shoreline. The Eastern New England Upland region covers northern, eastern, and central Maine. It consists of densely forested **plateaus**, with elevations ranging from 1,100 to 1,250 feet. Rivers, lakes, and **eskers** are also found in this region. The White Mountains Region occupies northwestern Maine. It has the state's highest mountains and thickest forests.

Maine experiences long, cold winters. Cold Arctic air from the Labrador Current prevents the warm air of the Gulf Stream from reaching the state. Heavy snowfalls are common. In 1998, two of the worst blizzards in the state's history occurred back to back. They left more than 400,000 people in Maine snowbound in their homes for up to three weeks.

During autumn, Maine's trees are ablaze with color.

QUICK FACTS

The highest point in Maine is Mount Katahdin, located in the central part of the state. It rises 5,268 feet above sea level. Maine has nine other peaks that rise above 4,000 feet.

Thousands of islands dot Maine's coast. Some are large enough to support thriving towns. The largest island is Mount Desert. It is home to Cadillac Mountain, which rises 1,530 feet.

January is Maine's snowiest month. At this time of year, the state receives an average of 20 inches of snow.

NATURAL RESOURCES

Trees are one of Maine's most important natural resources. There are 17 million acres of forest in the state. These forests supply raw materials for many of the wood products made in Maine. Private companies that harvest trees for lumber or paper production own most of Maine's forests. Many companies use tree farming and eco-management to maintain forest resources. These methods ensure that Maine's forests are preserved for future generations.

Water is another major natural resource. Maine has more than 5,000 rivers and streams. Many of these rivers can be used to produce **hydroelectricity**. Hydroelectric dams are found on the state's four major rivers—the Kennebec, the Penobscot, the Androscoggin, and the Saco. These dams produce about 50 percent of the state's total electricity. Maine also has about 6,000 lakes and ponds. The lakes and rivers along the coastal waters support a variety of fish and marine life.

Spruce, balsam fir, and white pine are the most commonly harvested trees in Maine.

The northeastern part of the state has soils that are ideal for potato farming.

QUICK FACTS

The largest lake in Maine is Moosehead Lake. It covers 117 square miles.

Maine's most valuable minerals are sand, gravel, and limestone.

The state gemstone is tourmaline. It is found in deposits of silica and comes in a variety of colors, including blue, green, and black.

PLANTS AND ANIMALS

A great number of tree species are found in the state's vast forests. In the north, spruce and fir thrive. Elsewhere, maple, birch, and white pine are common. Although private companies own most of Maine's forests, the state has created several designated wilderness areas. One such area is Baxter State Park. Located in northern Maine, this park protects about 200,000 acres of wilderness. Former governor Percival Baxter created the park in 1931. He wanted to ensure that a portion of Maine's beautiful wilderness remained natural.

Although the state is known for its number of trees, there are also many colorful wildflowers. Among them are asters, black-eyed Susans, and buttercups. Maine is also known for the many blueberry bushes that grow throughout the northern Coastal Lowlands. Lowbush blueberry shrubs are about 6 to 18 inches tall. Healthy plants can live longer than 50 years.

Ripe blueberries range in color from light to dark blue. They have a powdery-gray film.

Fireweed, commonly found in Maine, is one of the first plants to appear in a burned-over area. It grows up to 8 feet in height.

Moose have long legs which allow them to feed on low bushes and to wade in lakes and ponds to feed on aquatic plants.

Maine's forests and waters are home to a remarkable variety of wildlife. In fact, Maine has one of the most varied wildlife populations in the eastern United States. Among the state's many land animals are foxes, lynxes, chipmunks, and porcupines. More than 25,000 moose, Maine's state mammal, roam all over Maine. They thrive primarily in northern and western regions. Some moose can weigh up to 1,400 pounds, and their antlers alone can weigh up to 50 pounds. Moose are considered North America's tallest land mammal. They can often stand over 7 feet tall.

A wide range of marine life is found in Maine's coastal waters. Finback, humpback, and minke whales can all be seen in the Gulf of Maine. A minke whale has a curved dorsal fin and a white stripe on its flippers. Basking sharks and porpoises also live in these waters, as do a variety of shellfish such as lobsters, crabs, and shrimps. Harbor seals inhabit Maine's coastal waters.

QUICK FACTS

Basking sharks, found in the Gulf of Maine, are among the largest species of shark. They can often grow as long as 40 feet.

More than 300 bird species are found in Maine. They range from small birds such as sparrows and blue jays to predatory birds such as eagles and hawks. The state is also home to many water birds, including ducks, loons, herons, cormorants, and terns.

In the summer, Atlantic puffins can be seen on many islands off the coast of Maine, including Matinicus Isle.

Over thousands of years, water has carved Thunder Hole out of the rock on Maine's shores.

TOURISM

Sparkling lakes, rushing rivers, dense forests, towering mountains, and beautiful stretches of coastline all serve to make the state a natural paradise for vacationers. Many tourists travel to Maine to enjoy the recreational activities offered by wilderness areas such as Baxter State Park, White Mountain National Forest, and the Allagash Wilderness Waterway. Other tourists are drawn to the state's seaside villages and mountain communities.

Mount Desert Island is a popular tourist destination in Maine. Charming communities, historic inns, and remote country roads can be found on Mount Desert Island. The island's Acadia National Park encompasses nearly half of the island, as well as parts of the mainland. It offers a stunning landscape of rugged cliffs and rich woodlands. One of the most visited wonders in the park is a deep, coastal cavern called Thunder Hole. Seawater rushes into this cavern, compresses, then bursts out with an explosive force to a height of 40 feet and a roar like the sound of thunder.

The Mount Desert Oceanarium in Maine has a lobster hatchery and indoor tanks full of local sea life, such as sea urchins.

QUICK FACTS

Portland is home to the Children's Museum of Maine. This museum features a variety of fun displays, including a model space shuttle, a gigantic globe, a grocery store, and a lobster boat.

The town of Bath is home to the Maine Maritime Museum. The museum is located in a nineteenth-century shipyard where large wooden ships were once constructed. Displays inside the Maritime History Building include paintings, ship models, exhibits on life at sea, and maritime biology.

Fishers in Maine use lobster traps. Maine is the only state that does not drag the ocean floor for lobsters.

INDUSTRY

Maine's economy is linked to its abundant natural resources. Trees supply the raw materials for making paper products. The manufacture of paper is one of Maine's largest industries, and many major paper companies are based in the state. Great Northern Paper Inc. has pulp and paper mills in Millinocket, and employs more than 1,300 people. It specializes in paper for telephone directories. Maine's trees are also harvested for the manufacture of lumber. Sawmills and lumber camps are found all over the state. Other wood products manufactured in Maine include clothespins, lobster traps, matches, and toothpicks. In fact, about 90 percent of the country's toothpicks are made in Maine.

Fishing is another major industry in the state. Maine's coastal waters provide profitable catches of fish and shellfish. Maine's annual fish catch is valued at more than $250 million. The annual lobster catch is the largest in the nation. About 90 percent of the country's lobster supply is caught off the coast of Maine. As well, the state follows Maryland in the number of soft-shell clams harvested.

Maine has nearly 6,000 licensed lobster fishers.

Between 50 and 75 million pounds of blueberries are processed each year in Maine.

GOODS AND SERVICES

Agriculture is an important contributor to the state's economy. Maine ranks second in New England and about fifth in the country in potato production. Dairy products and eggs are among Maine's other leading agricultural items. Broccoli, peas, and dry beans also grow well in the state. As well, Maine is one of the world's leading producers of wild blueberries. The state produces about 98 percent of all the blueberries sold in the United States. Many of the state's fresh farm goods are responsible for a thriving food processing industry. Factories in Maine can and freeze vegetables and fruit.

Many of the goods produced in Maine are exported to other states and countries. Trucks transport the majority of Maine's freight. The state has a network of highways that provide easy access to other regions of the country. Portland also serves as Maine's major seaport. It handles a larger volume of freight than any other port in the state.

The Maine Maritime Academy was created in 1941.

QUICK FACTS

About fifty-five newspapers are published in Maine. The *Bangor Daily News* has the largest circulation.

Maine's very first radio station began broadcasting from Bangor in 1922. Today, there are about sixty radio stations.

Private colleges in Maine include Bowdoin College in Brunswick, Bates College in Lewiston, and Colby College in Waterville.

The first television station in Maine was established in Bangor in 1953. Today, about fifteen television stations are based in the state.

Maine's service industries employ the largest percentage of workers. Tourism is one of the largest service industries in Maine. Those in the tourism industry work at a variety of tourist attractions, such as hotels and museums.

Education is another important service in the state. During Maine's colonial days, students had limited access to formal education. For years, the only type of formal instruction available was provided by a moving school. This school traveled from one community to another, spending only a short time in each place. Today, Maine places great emphasis on the importance of education. It **allocates** more money to students and schools than most other states in the country. Maine also has many excellent colleges and universities, including the University of Maine, which was established in Orono in 1862. A rare kind of school, the Maine Maritime Academy, is located in Castine. The Maine Maritime Academy specializes in ocean and marine-oriented education, training students in areas such as ship operations, ocean management, and marine science.

Nearly 78,000 people in Maine work in the service industry.

Scientific evidence suggests that Paleo-Indians hunted large animals such as caribou and muskox.

FIRST NATIONS

Archeological discoveries in Maine have led scientists to believe that people were living in the state more than 10,000 years ago. Evidence suggests that these early peoples hunted caribou, muskox, and other large animals that are no longer found in Maine. Another group emerged in Maine about 4,000 years ago. They are known as the Red Paint Peoples because of their fascinating burial practices. They lined burial pits with bright red **ochre,** then placed unusual stone tools and weapons in the pits before burying their dead. The Red Paint Peoples thrived in the area until about 1800 BC.

When European explorers arrived in Maine in the sixteenth century, several groups of Native Peoples were living in the region. Most belonged to the Abenaki nation, including the Penobscot and the Passamaquoddy. The Native Peoples lost much of the land to the Europeans. In 1980, the United States government agreed to pay $81.5 million to Maine's Passamaquoddy, Penobscot, and Maliseet. The money was payment for land taken through illegal agreements in the 1800s.

QUICK FACTS

The word *Abenaki* means "people of the sunrise."

Scientists believe that when Europeans began settling in the Maine region, the Abenaki population was as high as 20,000. However, by 1620, this number was cut in half due to the new diseases that were spread by the settlers.

The Iroquois were fierce enemies of the Abenaki. Iroquois groups lived primarily to the west of Maine, but they would often travel east to raid Abenaki villages in the area.

The Mi'kmaq inhabited the eastern regions of Maine. They were also part of the Abenaki nation, but they often battled with other Abenaki groups.

Many early Native Peoples hunted porpoises off the shores of Maine.

Historians are still unable to determine whether Sebastian Cabot really sailed Maine's coast.

French and English
fur traders explored the Maine region during the early 1600s. Many of these Europeans established professional relationships with the Abenaki, trading items such as guns and kettles for beaver pelts and other furs.

Among the English
explorers sent to explore Maine were Bartholomew Gosnold in 1602, Martin Pring in 1603, and George Weymouth in 1605.

A French Jesuit mission
was established on Mount Desert Island in 1613. When the English commander of a Virginia Company fishing expedition discovered the mission, he ordered the Jesuits to leave. He then destroyed their settlement.

EXPLORERS AND MISSIONARIES

Maine's early history is uncertain. It is not known when the first European explorers reached Maine. Vikings, led by Leif Ericson, are thought to have visited Maine about 1100 AD. However, the only evidence to suggest their visit is a Norse coin that was discovered in 1961. There is also some doubt about whether an expedition led by John Cabot reached the Maine coast in 1497. Cabot's son, Sebastian, who was part of the expedition, claimed that they had sailed Maine's coast. Unfortunately, records kept during the expedition were unclear, leading many historians to question Sebastian's claim.

There is no doubt, however, that an Italian explorer named Giovanni de Verrazzano visited the region in the early sixteenth century. Sailing on behalf of France, de Verrazzano arrived on Maine's coast in 1524 and left precise reports. He soon left the area, but not before claiming it for France. Soon after, European fishers discovered Maine's excellent coastal fishing grounds, and more ships began to frequent the area's waters.

A gold coin discovered in Maine suggests that Norse explorers may have visited the area.

EARLY SETTLERS

At the beginning of the seventeenth century, both France and England attempted to establish colonies in Maine. In 1604, French explorers Pierre du Guast and Samuel de Champlain established a settlement along the Saint Croix River. However, after a harsh winter, the settlers left the area and founded a new colony in present-day Canada. In 1607, an English corporation called the Plymouth Company sent colonists to establish a settlement at the mouth of the Kennebec River. The settlement was named the Popham Plantation in honor of its leader, Sir John Popham. Like the French before them, the settlers of Popham Plantation suffered through a terrible winter. They returned to England in 1608.

In 1622, the Council of New England and King Charles I granted Maine and New Hampshire to Englishmen Ferdinando Gorges and John Mason. They divided the area in 1629. Gorges received the northeastern portion. Although he did not actually set foot in the area, Gorges established the first government in 1636. Soon after, in 1641, the community of Gorgeana became the first chartered English city. By 1650, permanent communities existed at Scarboro, Wells, Kettery, and York.

QUICK FACTS

The settlers of the Popham Plantation built a boat called *The Virginia* so that they could sail home to England. *The Virginia* was the first boat built by English colonists in the United States.

Ferdinando Gorges spent most of his adult life developing colonies in New England. Despite this devotion, Gorges never actually set foot in New England, nor did he ever visit any other region of North America.

Maine remained a part of Massachusetts for almost 150 years.

Some people in Maine wished to remain loyal to the English Crown during the American Revolution. They were known as Loyalists.

Samuel de Champlain attempted to name the Native Peoples that he came across in Maine.

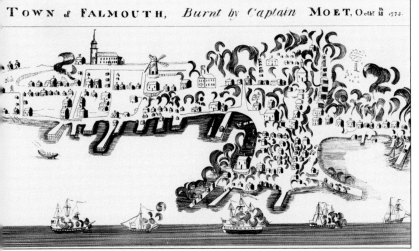

TOWN of FALMOUTH, *Burnt by Captain* MOET, *Octbr 18 1775*

During the American Revolution in 1775, British troops burned the town of Falmouth, which is now Portland, to punish the townspeople for opposing the king's policies.

Land disputes between England and France erupted into violent battles. From the late 1600s to the early 1700s, the two powers fought many wars for control of Maine and the rest of North America. In 1763, this turmoil came to an end with the **Treaty** of Paris, which declared that France was to give up all of its land claims in North America. Very soon after the treaty, England decided to increase the colonists' taxes and restrict their trade. These actions caused severe unrest among the colonists, and many decided to fight for their independence. In 1775, hundreds of Maine residents joined the American Revolution.

When the colonists emerged victorious in 1783, thirteen colonies came together to form the United States. At that time, Maine was considered part of Massachusetts, but a movement for separation began to gain strength. There were many supporters, and in 1819, Maine voted in favor of separation from Massachusetts. On March 15, 1820, with a population of about 300,000 people, Maine entered the Union as the twenty-third state. More settlers soon arrived to take advantage of the state's thriving industries.

QUICK FACTS

Maine's admission to the Union was part of the Missouri **Compromise**. This agreement allowed Maine to enter the Union as a **free state** and Missouri to enter as a slave state. Under the Missouri Compromise, the Union's number of free and slave states remained equal.

In 1851, Maine passed a law forbidding the production or sale of alcohol in the state.

Shipbuilding was a very important industry in many of Maine's coastal towns. Workers built clipper ships, schooners, and large commercial ships.

Portland, the largest city in Maine, was founded in 1632.

QUICK FACTS

Maine's most populated counties are Androscoggin, Cumberland, Penobscot, and York. They are all located in the southwestern part of the state.

Aroostook County covers 6,453 square miles, making it the largest county in the United States east of the Mississippi River.

More than half of Maine's population lives within 25 miles of the coast.

Maine's population has increased by about 4 percent since 1990.

There are only 41.3 people per square mile in Maine. This is much lower than the national average of almost 80 people per square mile.

POPULATION

Maine is home to 1.27 million people. The majority of these people live in towns or communities with populations of less than 2,500. Only 45 percent of Maine's population lives in one of the state's urban areas. This makes Maine one of the few states in the country where the rural population is higher than the urban population. The cities are small. Portland, with about 65,000 people, is Maine's largest city. Among the state's other cities are Lewiston-Auburn, Bangor, Augusta, Biddeford, and Waterville. More than half of the population lives in the southwest corner of Maine, leaving large portions of the state sparsely inhabited.

About 96 percent of the people living in Maine were born in the United States, and most are of European descent. People with English ancestry are by far the largest cultural group in Maine. However, people of French, Irish, French-Canadian, German, and Swedish descent are also present in significant numbers. Less than 1 percent of Maine's population is African American or Native American.

Each August, Brunswick holds the Maine Festival, which features Maine artists, performers, craftspersons, and vendors.

The Governor's offices, House of Representatives, and Senate Chambers are all housed inside the Maine Capitol.

POLITICS AND GOVERNMENT

Maine's government is made up of three branches. The legislative branch makes the state's laws. It consists of the Senate, which has 35 members, and the House of Representatives, which has 151 members. All members are elected to two-year terms. The executive branch of government ensures that the laws are carried out. This branch is headed by a governor who is elected to a four-year term. The governor is the only member of the executive branch who is elected by the people. Other members are chosen by the Legislature or appointed by the governor with approval from the Senate. The third branch of government is the judicial branch. It interprets the state's laws and ensures that they are obeyed.

Maine has sixteen counties, twenty-two cities, and 424 incorporated towns. Cities in Maine are run either by a mayor or a city manager.

QUICK FACTS

Maine still operates under its original constitution, which was adopted in 1819. Over the years, this constitution has been amended several times, but it has never been completely rewritten.

The Supreme Court is the highest court in the state.

Margaret Chase Smith, of Skowhegan, Maine, was the first woman ever to serve in both United States houses of Congress. She served in the House of Representatives from 1940 to 1949, and in the Senate from 1949 to 1973.

Maine has many levels of local government. Each of the state's counties elect three commissioners—an attorney, a sheriff, and a treasurer.

Margaret Chase Smith was the first woman to have her name placed in nomination for the presidency by either of the two major parties.

Since 1978, Madawaska has celebrated Acadian culture with a variety of traditional events, such as dancing.

CULTURAL GROUPS

Maine's people come from a variety of cultural backgrounds. The first Europeans to establish permanent settlements in Maine came from England. They were soon joined by English colonists who migrated to Maine from other states, and by Scots-Irish settlers. Together, the English and the Scots-Irish made up the largest portion of Maine's population during its early settlement days.

People of French descent make up the second-largest cultural group in Maine. In 1763, the English expelled French settlers, called Acadians, from Nova Scotia, Canada. Many of them established homes in the St. John Valley. In the nineteenth century, French Canadians from Quebec moved to Maine in order to find jobs in the lumber and textile mills. Today, Maine's French culture is recognized at the Acadian Historic Village in Van Buren. It features sixteen reconstructed buildings that depict early Acadian life in the St. John Valley. Among the buildings on display are a country schoolhouse, a blacksmith shop, and a chapel.

QUICK FACTS

French is the primary language spoken in most of the St. John Valley, and it is the second language spoken in many of Maine's cities.

Every June, the town of Madawaska celebrates Acadian heritage with the Acadian Festival. This festival has become one of the largest cultural events in Maine.

Many other European settlers came to Maine in the nineteenth century to work in the state's lumber and textile mills. Among these immigrants were Italians, Russians, Poles, and Finns.

Scottish bagpipers may be seen at the Bay Festival, held every July in Belfast.

The Abbe Museum has been open to the public since 1928.

In the mid-nineteenth century, people in Maine began to move westward to other states. In an effort to keep settlement numbers high, Maine's commissioner of immigration brought a group of fifty-one Swedish immigrants to the area in 1870. These immigrants established a colony in Aroostook County that soon grew into the township of New Sweden. Soon, the Swedish townships of Westmanland and Stockholm were established close by. Descendants of these early Swedish settlers continue to live in these communities. The New Sweden Museum boasts an original log house and blacksmith shop. Every summer, the community of New Sweden celebrates and shares its heritage with the Midsommar Celebration. The festival features Swedish food, music, and dancing.

Before any Europeans settled in Maine, many Native Peoples called the area home. Today, many of their descendants still live in the state. The Passamaquoddy live mostly on two reservations in Washington County, while the Penobscot live on Indian Island in the Penobscot River. There are also small populations of Mi'kmaq and Maliseet in Maine.

During the Midsommar Celebration, people, including children, dress up in traditional Swedish costumes.

Many of Stephen King's stories are set in a fictional town in Maine named Castle Rock.

ARTS AND ENTERTAINMENT

Maine's beauty has served as an inspiration for many poets and novelists. Henry Wadsworth Longfellow is considered to be one of the country's most influential poets. He was born in Portland in 1807, and later attended Bowdoin College. Among Longfellow's many admired poems are "The Song of Hiawatha" and "The Wreck of the Hesperus." Edna St. Vincent Millay was another popular poet from Maine. She was born in Rockland in 1892. In 1923, she received the Pulitzer Prize for a volume of poetry titled *The Harp-Weaver and Other Poems*.

Many novelists have lived in the state as well. These include such greats as Harriet Beecher Stowe, Kenneth Roberts, and Sarah Orne Jewett. One of the country's most popular **contemporary** novelists is also from Maine. Stephen King was born in Portland and currently lives in Bangor. He is known for his chilling horror novels that feature ordinary characters who must battle against evil forces. Among his many bestsellers are *The Shining*, *Pet Cemetery*, and *Bag of Bones*. Several of his novels have been made into popular Hollywood movies.

QUICK FACTS

Henry Wadsworth Longfellow's poem "Evangeline" traces the story of the Acadians and their forced deportation.

Poet Edwin Arlington Robinson was born in Head Tide, Maine in 1869. Some of his most popular poems include "Miniver Cheevy," "Richard Cory," and "The Tree in Pamela's Garden." He was awarded the Pulitzer Prize three times for his work.

Harriet Beecher Stowe wrote her first novel, *Uncle Tom's Cabin*, while living in Brunswick, Maine in 1852. This anti-slavery masterpiece is often said to have helped trigger the Civil War.

E. B. White spent many of his summers at Penobscot Bay. White is perhaps best known for his popular children's novels, *Stuart Little* and *Charlotte's Web*.

In addition to poetry, Edna St. Vincent Millay wrote several plays for an experimental theater group called the Provincetown Players.

In the summer, many people participate in the Bay Festival Parade in Belfast.

Maine's stunning natural scenery has also inspired many visual artists. Renowned painters, such as Thomas Cole, Winslow Homer, Rockwell Kent, Edward Hopper, and Andrew Wyeth, have all captured the state's peaceful way of life and its rugged, beautiful landscapes on canvas. Other artists have represented Maine's beauty through photographs, sculptures, and craftwork. Many of the works produced in Maine are on display in galleries, such as the Portland Museum of Art and the Bowdoin Museum of Art in Brunswick.

Exciting theatrical performances and musical events take place in Maine each year. Maine is also home to a wide range of talented musical groups, from barbershop quartets to choral music choirs. Many of the state's musical groups and theatrical troupes take part in the Maine Festival. This festival takes place every summer in Brunswick and celebrates Maine's creative spirit. There are eight stages featuring a variety of performances, such as music, dance, literary readings, and theater.

The Blue Hill Brass Band plays at the Bay Festival in Belfast.

Kayaks are completely enclosed with an opening for the kayaker to sit in. This keeps the kayaker warm and dry in Maine's chilly waters.

QUICK FACTS

The Allagash Wilderness Waterway is a popular canoe route. It consists of a 92-mile corridor of lakes and rivers with many camping areas.

The Annual Maine Potato Blossom Festival at Fort Fairfield features unique athletic events such as potato picking contests and mashed potato wrestling.

SPORTS

A variety of water sports may be enjoyed in Maine's coastal waters, lakes, and rivers. Sea kayakers paddle along the state's beautiful coastline and explore the offshore islands and protected **estuaries**. Surfers are also attracted to Maine's coast. The area's large, crashing **breakers** provide excellent challenges for experienced surfers. Beautiful ocean beaches in the southern part of the state buzz with activity. These coastal waters are quite chilly, and swimming is not for everyone. Warmer waters are found in Maine's lakes. Other water sports enjoyed in Maine include canoeing, whitewater rafting, and **windjamming**.

Excellent hiking and biking trails are found in Maine's mountains and forests. One of the most popular hikes is the Appalachian National Scenic Trail, which begins in Maine near Mount Katahdin. This trail winds more than 2,000 miles through the Appalachian Mountains and crosses fourteen states. The Maine section of the Appalachian Trail has steep climbs and dense woods that provide a great hiking challenge.

Its proximity to the ocean has helped Maine earn a highly respected reputation in surfing.

Although winter in Maine is usually long and cold, many sports enthusiasts consider it to be the state's best season. Once the first few snowfalls have blanketed the state, Maine's hiking and biking trails turn into excellent areas for snowshoeing, snowmobiling, and cross-country skiing. Ice skating and ice fishing are popular activities when Maine's lakes and ponds have frozen over, and frozen waterfalls provide slippery challenges for ice climbers.

Downhill skiing is probably Maine's most popular winter sport. The state boasts twenty-five ski hills. The two major ski resorts are Sugarloaf and Sunday River. Both have a variety of runs that are suitable for skiers and snowboarders of all ability levels. Among the state's other great hills are Shawnee Peak, Saddleback, Big Rock, and Lost Valley. Maine's ski hills play host to a variety of ski and snowboard events, including the Snowboard Big Air Competition at Lost Valley, the Telemark World Cup at Sugarloaf, and the Sprint US Freestyle Grand National World Cup at Sunday River.

Tobogganing is a fun way to spend a winter day in Maine.

Maine has 12,000 miles of groomed snowmobiling trails.

Brain Teasers

1 TRUE OR FALSE?

Augusta has always been the capital of Maine.

Answer: False. Portland served as the state capital until 1832.

2 MULTIPLE CHOICE:

One of the landmarks in Kennebunk is a house that was constructed to resemble a:

a. Boat   b. Pine Tree

c. Wedding Cake   d. Shoe

Answer: c. In the mid-1800s, a retired sea captain named George Bourne covered his house and barn with detailed woodcarvings that resembled the design of a fancy wedding cake.

3 TRUE OR FALSE?

Earmuffs were invented in Maine.

Answer: True. Chester Greenwood, a 15 year-old boy from Farmington, invented the world's first earmuffs in 1873.

4 TRUE OR FALSE?

The largest wooden ship ever built in the United States was constructed in Maine.

Answer: True. Called The Wyoming, this wooden ship was built in 1904 in the shipyards that now house the Maine Maritime Museum. The Wyoming measured 324 feet in length.

5

TRUE OR FALSE?

The United States and Canada almost went to war over disputes concerning Maine's border with New Brunswick.

Answer: True. After the American Revolution, many heated disputes took place over the location of the border. The disputes came to a head in 1839 when both sides sent troops to defend what is now known as Aroostook County.

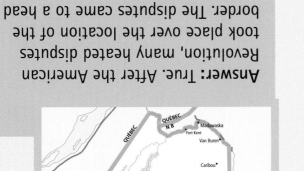

6

MULTIPLE CHOICE:

How many politicians from Maine have served as vice-president of the United States?

a. Zero

b. Two

c. Five

d. Seven

Answer: b. Two. Vice-Presidents Hannibal Hamlin and Nelson Aldrich Rockefeller were both from Maine.

7

MAKE A GUESS:

What Maine city has been known as Machigonne, Elbow, The Neck, Casco, and Falmouth over the years?

Answer: Portland. It received its current name after the American Revolution.

8

TRUE OR FALSE?

Lobster has been used as fertilizer in Maine.

Answer: True. Lobster was so common in the eighteenth century that it was used as fertilizer.

FOR MORE INFORMATION

Books

Leamon, James S., *Revolution Downeast: The War for American Independence in Maine.* Massachusetts: University of Massachusetts Press, 1995.

McLane, Charles B., and McLane, Carol Everts, *Islands of the Mid-Maine Coast: Penobscot Bay.* Maine: Tilbury House Publishers, 1997.

Paine, Lincoln P., et al, *Down East: A Maritime History of Maine.* Maine: Tilbury House Publishers, 2000.

Web Sites

You can also go online and have a look at the following Web sites:

Government of Maine
http://www.state.me.us

Government of Maine Kid's Page
http://www.state.me.us/sos/kids

Visit Maine
http://www.visitmaine.com

Acadia National Park
http://www.nps.gov/acad/home.htm

Some Web sites stay current longer than others. To find other Maine Web sites, enter search terms such as "New England," "Bangor," "Portland," or any other topic you want to research.

GLOSSARY

allocates: set something, such as money, aside for a particular purpose

aquaculture: fish farming

breakers: a wave that breaks into foam

compromise: a settlement

contemporary: modern, present-day

eco-tourism: tourism to places having unspoiled natural resources

eskers: winding ridges of gravel and other sediment, formed by glacial meltwater

estuaries: the tidal area where a river meets the sea

free state: a state where slavery is not permitted

hydroelectricity: electricity generated by the power of moving water

Jesuit: a Roman Catholic order of priests

ochre: clay that is orange or red in color

plateaus: raised land areas that have a fairly level surface

treaty: an agreement

windjamming: sailing on a large ship

INDEX